The Marriage Mentor

5 Ways to Reduce Friction, Increase Communication and Restore Harmony

By

Bethany Shields

2ndEmpireMedia.Com

INTRODUCTION

Why do we fight anyway?
Disagreements and heated discussions are inevitable in any relationship, especially when two different individuals from two different backgrounds and upbringings move in together to start their happily ever after fairy tale life as husband and wife. Up until then, there is infatuation, excitement, and dreams of connecting with their soul mate forever as they ride into the sunset together. Been there? Done that?
Many of us realize shortly after the "I do's" that maybe you shouldn't have. It could be a number of things that cause you to rethink your decision.

Guys often enjoy the hunt and victory of capturing the girl of their dreams, but soon realize they just made a commitment to "forsake all others." Initially, this seems impossible since "playing the field" has been their mode of operation for so long.
Fear then creeps in just thinking about switching to a monogamous mentality, starting with changing their status on all social media platforms to "married."

An overwhelmed feeling follows as they contemplate what's required: (1) letting go of independence and working towards interdependence; (2) sharing their time, space, income, and stuff for a greater good; and (3) embarking on the journey of learning and relating based on the temperament and love language of their lifelong partner.

Of course the benefits of marriage help calm some of his nerves: the love of his life will be by his side through thick and thin; the memories they make together will be lasting and more meaningful, especially as they add kids; and having someone to share intimate moments with, as well as having a committed love that is bonding and promotes their 'ever after' together.

Gals, on the other hand, see things very differently. For most women, finding the love of her life and marrying him is just the beginning of her dreams coming true. She looks forward to being romanced by her Prince Charming daily, she envisions doing everything together with her soul mate, and she hopes for children to complete the family.

She is excited to change her status to "married" and will post and tweet tons of selfies with her forever friend. If she had a positive experience with her parents, especially her dad, she will desire her new partner to continue the legacy, but if she didn't, she will probably have higher or lofty expectations of her husband.
Intimacy is spelled differently for her than for him.
It is spelled T-A-L-K, not S-E-X.

Her emotions are the gateway to physical intimacy, and the physical is the gateway to his emotions. These differences – there are many, many more – spark conflicting feelings, enlists verbal and non-verbal communiqués, and begins to reveal the character and intentions of both husband and wife.

Depending on their temperament and environment when confronted with an opposing idea, the couple will either resolve issues quickly – compromising and learning from each other, or will allow one person's opinion to prevail to avoid a confrontation – sweeping issues under the rug, or will butt heads until the master manipulator has his/her way – often causing hurt feelings and resentment to build. I agree with Dr. Phil's statement, "Fighting is a part of any relationship.

You are not ever going to merge or share your life with someone and not have conflict. There is plenty of adjustment. It's not whether you fight that's going to determine the success or failure of your relationship; it's how you fight."

This is the objective of this book: to help couples learn how to fight in a way that builds up their marriage and relationship instead of chipping away at it until it falls apart. I firmly believe that all marriages have their share of highs and lows in their journey together.

I advocate that the couple that achieves more highs than lows is much more satisfied and happy in their marriage than those with more lows. These highs don't come naturally; they require intentionality, fueled with love and commitment. Couples need proven and real-life strategies to overcome conflict and come away with a high! I concur that makeup-sex is great, but it'll be even sweeter if you are able to resolve issues and rebuild trust for each other.

Am I advising you to have more arguments in order to create more highs so your marriage will soar? Of course not! But I am suggesting that since you will have conflict, you might as well learn how to effectively capitalize on these marital strengthening opportunities.

In this book, you will learn "Five Ways to Reduce Fighting in Your Marriage" in order to maximize these opportunities and motivate you towards your 'ever after.' But before we jump into the ring, I'd like you to consider a few fighting principles:

1. **Your spouse is not your enemy or adversary, but is your partner and teammate.** Often, once in the midst of conflict, we forget this important distinction. So instead of going in for the kill, you should focus on how to improve one another and your marriage. Keeping this in mind, make sure you treat him/her better than you would a co-worker or friend.

Remember, he/she is your 'for better or worse' friend to the end. In order to go the distance with him/her, you need to make sure you're building each other up rather than tearing down your forever friend.

2. Don't strive for the win or draw; rather, go for the 'win-win!' Just think about it, when one wins, one loses.
This definitely does not boost morale, nor does it grow relationships. So even if you happen to be more right at the moment, avoid gloating and doing a fist pump.

Rather, affirm and demonstrate exceptional love to your spouse. Remember, you might be right this time, but might not be right the next time. If you continue to 'one-up' each other, you will become fixated on 'me' instead between you two. Look for the 'win-win' and you'll grow and nurture your love connection for years to come.

3. When you begin engaging in battle, remember that the quicker you resolve issues, the better off you will be personally and as a couple. I'm sure you've let something fester a while – we all have – so you already know how you lose sleep, how you are easily irritated, and you become self-protecting. Regain perspective.

Remaining calm, caring, and patient with one another will help diffuse and resolve issues quicker than if you allow heated emotions to enter into your debate.

These are the keys to turn your fighting IN your marriage into fighting FOR your marriage.

Now let's consider Five Ways to Reduce Fighting in Your Marriage. Are you *'All In for the Win-Win'?*

CHAPTER ONE

Put Up Your Dukes!

What is causing the quarrels and fights among you? Don't they come from the evil desires at war within you? 2 You want what you don't have, so you scheme and kill to get it. You are jealous of what others have, but you can't get it, so you fight and wage war to take it away from them. Yet you don't have what you want because you don't ask God for it.

And even when you ask, you don't get it because your motives are all wrong—you want only what will give you pleasure. James 4:1-3. There are certain givens in life: you are born and you will die; you sow and you will reap; and you will agree and disagree.

Why not live our lives intentionally in order to make the most of things inevitable? For instance, while we have no control over when and where we will be born, we do have control of how well we play the hand dealt to us, to the best of our abilities.

Also, knowing that we will reap the consequences of the decisions we make in life, why not take the time to think through the people we associate with, the directions in life we choose, and the one we select to marry and make a future with?

And finally, since we know there will be times we disagree with our spouse, shouldn't we learn how to turn polarizing differences into complementary compromises? When we consider the bigger picture of life, we will be able to manufacture marital highs over and over again.

The reality is, we are more into ourselves than our spouse.

We are more into getting what I want out of life than what our potential is as a couple. We are more interested in making a name for 'me' rather than 'we.' Self-centeredness, self-protection, and selfishness often prevail. It's no wonder at the time of this publication, 'selfies' are as big a deal as it is.

Not only can anyone take a selfie with their smart phone or tablet and post it on their favorite social media platform, there's even contests and a television sitcom based on the selfie phenomenon! We are totally into ourselves.

This internal obsession with 'me' is at the root of the above passage by James. Why do we fight? He says,
1. Selfish desires from within
2. You don't have, so you kill
3. You covet and don't get what you want
4. You pray to God and don't receive, because your motives are selfish

Selfish desires from within

Whether you adhere to biblical perspectives or not, you can't help but know what James is talking about and you know he's hit the nail on the proverbial head. Of course there are more reasons why we fight, but this is a good list of internal struggles of the 'selfie.'

I can totally relate with the first point. I see it over and over again. Wives going through their premenopausal season in life begin experiencing diminished sexual desires. So much so, that I have renamed this season in life, "men-on-pause!"

Many men work at putting pizzazz back between the sheets. They will beg, barter, and badger shamelessly. Even Christian husbands pull out their bibles to try to place a heavenly guilt trip to 'get it on.'

Here's a popular one;
"Now regarding the questions you asked in your letter. Yes, it is good to abstain from sexual relations. 2 But because there is so much sexual immorality, each man should have his own wife, and each woman should have her own husband.

The husband should fulfill his wife's sexual needs, and the wife should fulfill her husband's needs. The wife gives authority over her body to her husband, and the husband gives authority over his body to his wife. Do not deprive each other of sexual relations, unless you both agree to refrain from sexual intimacy for a limited time so you can give yourselves more completely to prayer.

Afterward, you should come together again so that Satan won't be able to tempt you because of your lack of self-control."
1 Corinthians 7:1-4 Who dare argue with God's authoritative word? Isn't it clear? "To avoid potential affairs, couples should not deprive each other sexually." Makes sense to me. After all, who even mentions they want to take a break for extended prayer times?

Whoa! Can you see what's happening? God's instructions shouldn't be used as a tool to pound the husband's agenda over their hormone stricken wives. God's intention for His Word is to cultivate love and oneness through intimacy – emotionally, spiritually, and physically. Yes, this passage should remind wives about fulfilling their marital duty, but it isn't up to husbands to manipulate their wives.

This is definitely not a loving and servant-leader move. While husbands are able to connect emotionally better once the physical needs are met, wives are the opposite. So who's more important in this instance? From his perspective, his wife should be, and from her perspective, her husband should be.

If they were both considering the needs of each other as more important than our own, 'self' would be left out of the picture, and they would be able to figure out the best course of action to take at the moment. Then it would result in true love-making instead of just having sex to fulfill an obligation. Win-Win!

You don't have, so you kill
The next 'why we fight principle' is, "You don't have, so you kill." Sounds pretty drastic, but just think about it. When we are deprived of something we expect or feel we deserve, we attack to obtain or reclaim our territory! Depending on our fighting style, we will lash out to claim our prize or possibly react passive-aggressively. Let's unpack four major styles of fighting:

The Aggressor. *Motto: "Win at all cost."* This is a very familiar fighting style. It is actually glorified on television and in the movies. The most aggressive, angry, and vocal person hurts others to get their way. They shout, swear, have fits of rage, raise their hands, push and shove, and get in your face in order to manipulate the situation in their favor.

This 'survival of the fittest' mentality is damaging for relationships. Often this style desires closer relations, but they actually push people away, and eventually isolate themselves. Even Charles Darwin, who coined the 'survival of the fittest' phrase said, "It is not the strongest or the most intelligent who will survive but those who can best manage change."

The Avoider. *Motto: "Peace at all cost."* Often paired with an Aggressor, the Avoider will do whatever they can to bypass any conflict. They even think of themselves as peace-loving citizens, forgiving and forgetting easily by sweeping things under the rug. But these well intentioned folks eventually have to face the music, most likely encountering multiple encores until the 'dissonants' are resolved.

Their peace breaks into pieces and it's usually harder to put together too. George St. Pierre said, "For me, personally, when I'm afraid of something - when you're afraid of something, normally you try to go away, you try to avoid it. Instead of avoiding it, to overcome your fear, I believe you need to embrace it."

The Avenger. *Motto: "Subtle at all cost."* Instead of embracing it, the Avenger will withdraw, stew in the matter, and then lash out in subtle ways. Avengers are experts in subtle combat strategies. Some are premeditated, but others are just from a mean streak from within.

Examples of subtle warfare tactics include, but are not limited to; sarcasm, negativity, procrastination, intentional lateness or laziness, and stubbornness. Within the marriage, the avenging partner can also withhold affection, assistance, and appreciation to create distance and dissatisfaction.

Instead of working towards a resolution of an issue, the Avenger will use his/her energies to hurt their partner in subtle ways.

The Assembler. *Motto: "Resolve at all cost."* Thank God for Assemblers! Instead of thinking of themselves, Assemblers are more interested in the big picture, the greater good, and their 'ever after.' So they sacrifice their comfort zone in order to resolve issues to keep their 'love boat' afloat and sailing towards their dream marriage.

They are not satisfied with the status quo or just surviving in their marriage. They want it to thrive, seeking to live happily ever after. That's why they work hard at resolving conflict as soon possible.

When we don't have what we want when we want it, we have a variety of ways of killing our spouse's self-esteem, killing a special moment, killing our trust factor, or killing our oneness quotient. Instead, strive to go against your normal tendencies and become an Assembler, resolving your relationship issues at all cost!

Understanding your fighting styles will help you turn your opponent into a sparring partner that will help you hone and grow your marriage, working to create more win-wins instead of knock outs.

You covet and don't get what you want

Coveting means to earnestly desire and long for something or someone that belongs to another. King David in the bible is someone most people know about that coveted someone else's wife, the beautiful Bathsheba.

How did he arrange this? He had an affair with her and then sent her husband to the front lines of battle where her husband paid the ultimate price. This made Bathsheba available. David coveted and got what he wanted, but suffered the consequences of his actions for the rest of his life despite the mercy, grace, and forgiveness that God gave him for that offense.

But not all of us have the resources that King David had at his disposal, so when we find ourselves coveting and not getting what we want, we struggle within and then will fight for it in a variety of ways. This is what James is referring to.

We could adopt the Aggressor or Avoider styles, or we can emulate David's premeditative strikes to acquire what we covet. Doesn't sound too good, right? But when we are impassioned, we sometimes stop thinking rationally.

Even in God's Top 10, not coveting anything or anyone that belongs to your neighbor is number 10. Why? Within the context of the Ten Commandments, coveting is one way to ruin relationships with one another.

When you consider His two summary commandments are to "Love God and Love Others," trying to possess another's someone or something violates the intent of the command and causes rifts between one another. Instead, we should cultivate what's in our own 'garden' and be happy and content with the produce we are blessed with.

You pray to God and don't receive, because your motives are selfish
God is in the business of answering the prayers of His people. However, if you were to study about prayer in the bible, you will be reminded that God is *not* a genie that grants your every wish, but a Loving Father that provides you with what you need for the

moment. His main conditions for answered prayer are; praying within His will and praying for things consistent with His heart's desire. And the way you learn how to do this is to remain close to Him and develop an abiding relationship with Him.

Here's a cool verse from Jesus' heart to ours:
"Yes, I am the vine; you are the branches. Those who remain in me, and I in them, will produce much fruit. For apart from me you can do nothing… But if you remain in me and my words remain in you, you may ask for anything you want, and it will be granted! When you produce much fruit, you are my true disciples. This brings great glory to my Father." John 15:5-8

He will answer our prayers because we are close to Him and we will ask what's close to His heart. This shows we are followers of Him and this brings glory to Him! Let me illustrate this important prayer principle like this: Remember when you were in high school?

You had about six different subjects with six different teachers, right? You knew that in order to be successful in each class, you not only had to know the material, but you also had to understand your teacher's styles and preferences.

As you watched and observed how he/she taught and interacted with you and your classmates, you learned to adjust your study skills and how to relate with each teacher to get the best grades possible. If you did not take the time to adjust to their ways and rules, you would not succeed in their class.

Similarly, we need to know God and understand His ways and means. We need to discern His reasons for where He's placed us and why, and then maximize our situations. We need to read, learn, and apply His Word into our lives so we can understand His best for our lives.

As we do this, we will grasp what's in His heart for our lives individually and as a couple, for His church (all followers of His Way), and the world at large. Then we will pray more effectively, less selfishly, and get answers. And even if His answers are "No" or "Wait", we will be understanding and persevere.

So instead of shaking a clinched fist at the Almighty for not granting your every wish, realize that you need to reassess your closeness to God and better gauge what His heartbeat is. Here are other thoughts from our contemporaries...

According to Dr. Steven Stosny in an article in Psychology Today, "Lovers fight when they believe their partners don't care about how they feel. They fight about the pain of disconnection. Disconnection occurs most frequently in intimate relationships when fear or anxiety in one causes a sense of inadequacy in the other."

The feeling of fear and anxiousness because of disconnectedness and inadequacies can be resolved when someone takes the initiative to mend the hurts through communication, forgiveness, and second chances. And if you are having difficulty working through an issue by yourselves, I highly recommend seeking out a marriage mentor or coach.
Take care of it early on when it's smaller!

According to **WE tv's Marriage Bootcamp** hosts, Jim and Elizabeth Carroll, "Statistics show that it ends up being money and then chores and everything, but what it really ends up being is couples get mad or angry at each other and they let a little bit of anger and resentment grow," he said. "And that gets in place and it blocks the love between them."

This is why it is better to nip things in the bud rather than to let it bloom into a bigger problem. If you haven't watched an episode of "Marriage Bootcamp," watch one on You Tube. You will see couples who failed to address issues early on in their relationship and it became a hot button that they continue to push.

And don't forget, it's a lot harder to work through the issues when they're big, rather than when the issues are smaller and more manageable.

Here are two more tips on turning your fighting 'in' your marriage to fighting 'for' your marriage. In the process of fighting…

Don't hit below the belt!
As mentioned earlier, it's normal for two different people from two different backgrounds and upbringing to disagree and fight. It is understanding why and how each other fights that's important.

But while engaging in battles, please realize that if someone 'wins,' the other 'loses,' and if there's a loser, you have lost as a couple. That being said, it is very important that you are always looking for the 'win-win' when you fight. And you will never obtain a 'win-win' when you hit below the belt!

What does that look like? Well, have you ever told your spouse that they were "stupid, lazy, worthless, or ugly?" That's hitting below the belt. Have you ever said it was their entire fault or that they made you do what you did? That's hitting below the belt. Or have you brought up past hurts or behaviors that weren't fully resolved?

That's hitting below the belt too. Here's Dr. Phil again, "Do they end it with character assassination, name calling, accusations and ridicule, not allowing their partner to retreat with dignity? Or do they end it in a constructive way looking for a solution?" That's right, Dr. Phil, is the couple constantly aiming below the belt or aiming for a win-win solution?

Another thing to remember is that whatever comes out of your mouth can't be taken back! The damage will be done no matter how much you apologize and repent afterwards. Words leave deep emotional scars that often take years to heal.

There's a great verse in the bible that says,
"Don't use foul or abusive language. Let everything you say be good and helpful, so that your words will be an encouragement to those who hear them." Ephesians 4:29

Wouldn't it be great if the things you tell people make a positive impression on them instead of a negative one? And wouldn't it be awesome if the positive impressions would lead to great achievements? Of course the opposite can be true too – leaving a negative impression that leads to a devastating outcome.

Which one do you choose for your soul mate, your best friend, your forever partner? Don't hit him/her below the belt!
Here's another…

Fight within the boundaries

What should marital boundaries be anyway? When we watch a boxing match, boxers must stay within the ring and adhere to the referee's instructions. When a boxer is down, he/she is allowed a 10-count before resuming while the other boxer goes to their corner. And of course, there's no hitting below the belt, as we already mentioned.

Another rule is, when the referee breaks you from a clinch, you have to take a full step back; you cannot immediately hit your opponent—that's called "hitting on the break" and is illegal. In other words, avoid always getting the last zinger in before you take a break. Illegal move!

Wouldn't it be wise to set up boundaries or rules for fighting within the marital ring? As mentioned earlier, our goal is not a knock out or a draw, but for two winners to come out of the ring together! That is what this book is all about, providing

Five **Ways to Reduce Fighting in Your Marriage** for couples of all ages and stages of life.
Check out these 10 Rules for Fair Fighting from the *#staymarried* blog:
1. No name calling
2. No interrupting
3. No blaming or accusations
4. No cursing
5. No yelling
6. No sarcasm
7. No defensiveness
8. No generalizations (you always, you never)
9. No physical/emotional intimidating gestures/violence/threats
10. No walking out without naming a follow up time

Here's one more that needs to be emphasized…
Stay on topic!

With emotions raging and defensive posturing taking place at the same time, it's easy to get off the subject and get on trails that would scare even the rabbits!

Make an agreement that if you do stray onto a rabbit trail, anyone is allowed to stop the conversation and remind each other of what the topic is. It would be honoring if someone writes down the secondary issue to be handled at a later date.

Coaching Tip #1:
Create a signal or code word that you two can recognize in the heat of the moment that can help you get back on track and can cool off a hot topic. Make it a ridiculous word, phrase, or gesture, one that will guarantee to make you smile. Something like, "Okay, it's time to get naked!" "Engelburt Humperdinck!" Or anything else that will make you smile.

Then pause, regroup, calm down, and start working through the issue at hand – until resolved! Works every time! To review, the first way to reduce fighting in your marriage is to fight with the 'win-win' in mind – to take conflicting moments and turn them into constructive intimacy building opportunities, to understand what your fighting styles are and use them for 'better' instead of 'worse', to handle the issues as they come rather than letting them fester and grow into monstrous proportions, don't hit below the belt or on the break, and avoid rabbit trails by staying on topic.

CHAPTER TWO

Hear No Evil, Speak No Evil, See No Evil

A day before I started writing this chapter, my wife and I were just chipping away at each other – defensive and offended easily about the littlest things. It was unnerving, irritating, and frustrating. I was really trying to respond correctly (since I coach couples on how to do this, right?) so I tried keeping quiet so as not to throw fuel on the fire, but she wanted me to respond, not be quiet.

I didn't want to do or say the wrong thing, so I felt like I was walking on eggshells! I shared with her that I understood that she wasn't feeling 100% because of the cough she'd been fighting and that she's been very busy and stressed about a variety of things. I also shared my frustration that even as a marriage coach I haven't been able to do and say the right things.

We looked at each other and realized that, as Christians, this was probably a spiritual attack by Satan who loves to see couples fight. So we apologized and forgave each other. Amazingly, the atmosphere changed, and we were back to normal. The next day, I opened my computer to write, and looked at the title of this chapter, and realized that while Satan meant that encounter for evil, God will use it for good! So here we go!

Assume the best in your spouse. This is a very important underlying principle for marriage. Remember while dating, your future spouse could do no wrong? Even the silly, stupid, and questionable things he/she did were endearing to you, even though they were 'red flags' to your friends.

The truth was those rose colored glasses helped your infatuation cover a multitude of sins. As years passed beyond your honeymoon, those rose colored glasses converted to magnifying glasses, where you were able to see every little flaw of your mate!

In this chapter, it is my desire for you to take those glasses – not rose colored or magnifying – and convert them to 'grace covered glasses.'

These special glasses will enable you to see your forever partner through the loving lenses of God – real and raw, yet realizing he/she is still in the process. Assuming the best in your spouse will 'jazz up' your marriage and enable you to 'hear no evil.'

Hear No Evil
There are two main ways to 'hear no evil' when relating to your spouse; when hearing about him/her and when listening to what he/she says.

Whenever someone tells you something about your spouse, especially when it's not favorable, this is when you can honor your spouse by not quickly accepting the news mentioned. Always relay a favorable response to your messenger and then hear what your spouse has to say.

Assume the best, similar to the axiom, "innocent before proven guilty." It is a cultural phenomenon, though, that we are quick to judge with feelings based on impressions, rather than with "the whole truth and nothing but the truth."

What this means in the courtroom is:
- the truth - what the witness experienced
- the whole truth - not leaving any material out
- nothing but the truth - definitely no lies

Besides assuming the best of your spouse, you have to realize that the other person will probably not have all the pertinent information to draw a conclusion or the information has already passed through several ears and mouths. And we all know that old proverb, "An open mouth gathers feet." So isn't having an open conversation with your spouse to clear the air the best thing to do? Afterwards, you can choose to explain the truth to your friend if you want.

But make sure you speak in general terms rather than in details to avoid feeding the rumor mill and possibly disrespecting your spouse. Show your friend that you are supportive of your spouse, even though the result of your conversation was not as good as you hoped. Which leads me to the next point…

Hear no evil when listening to your spouse. I know this is not as easy as it sounds. Personally, I really have to concentrate and choose to activate my loving listening skills. You can find lots of practical tips on developing listening skills in articles like, "10 Steps to Effective Listening," by Diane Schilling on the Forbes website. However, I would like to cover something that will allow you to communicate on a deeper more intimate level – listening with your heart, not just your ears.

When you listen to not hear any evil, you must listen beyond words, between the lines, and to their heart's intent. After all, the heart or essence of the person you married is what really drew you to them in the first place.

I've heard many people I've coached say that the person they're struggling with now is not the person they knew before. When he/she shares their heart with you, try keeping their words within the context of their heart, not just what was said. Be understanding and try to hear the words that aren't being communicated – what they are really trying to say & what they really need.

This is especially true for interracial couples. Watch for cues from their body language and tone of voice. This takes a lot of love and patience, so it would be wise to set a time when you are not distracted or exhausted and can devote all of your attention to the subject at hand. Feel the freedom to help each other out for maximum communication.

This takes practice – trial and error – but when you start getting this down, you will see your emotional and physical intimacy improve as well! This is actually a great idea for a Date Night!

Coaching Tip #2:
On a Date Night, commit to talking about "listening with your ears and heart." Guys, this will be a stretch for you because women are used to doing this. But take this opportunity to listen and learn from an expert. Ask thoughtful questions to make the intangible terms tangible for you.

Even if you walk away with a couple of things to think about and try the next time you converse, this is a win! Gals, it will seem you are speaking a foreign language to your man, so be aware of this and talk in terms they will understand. The fact that they are sitting in front of you should communicate their love for you and their desire to grow in this area of Hearing No Evil.

Speak No Evil
Again, biblical author, James, had some great advice for improving communication between couples, *"You must all be quick to listen, slow to speak, and slow to get angry." James 1:19*

Being quick to listen, while being slow to speak and getting angry. We have two ears, and one mouth. That's a good way to remember this. Listen first! And as I mentioned earlier, listen within the context of their heart.

Ask questions of clarification, repeat a summary of what you believe they said, affirm their courage to speak truth, and then speak to not 'win', but to achieve a 'win-win!'

The Apostle Paul, a contemporary of James, said, "Don't use foul or abusive language. Let everything you say be good and helpful, so that your words will be an encouragement to those who hear them." Ephesians 4:29

Be loving and respectful in word, body language, and behavior. You can employ *Gary Chapman's "The Five Love Languages"* to help even more. For instance, if your partner's love language is touch, make sure you place your hand softly on their shoulder, arm, or thigh whenever you speak with them.

If your partner's love language is affirmation, communicate to him/her appreciation for what they are doing well at the moment.
If your partner's love language is service, see what you can do to serve them as you talk. They will feel your love for them while relieving their stress level and tension.

Read his book to gain more insight into how to love in your spouse's dialect.

Being slow to speak will be more difficult for some than others. For those of you who are super articulate and are able to construct your thoughts quickly and on the fly, learning to be slow to speak when speaking with your spouse will be a challenge, but necessary.

If your work requires the former, by all means use those skills there. But at home, you need to be slow to speak in order to hear you lover's heart. Remember, you can raise your voice to be heard, but you can't raise your heart's volume. So you have to be quiet and attentive.

Gals, may I whisper into your ears for a minute? If you are the type I just described, it is important for your man to not feel more insecure in your marriage than he already is. Trust me on this, if you tone this area down and become slower to speak and quicker to listen to him, in time, your husband's confidence level will grow. The respect you are showing him will be the fertilizer that will geminate him into the man of your dreams!

Yes, he will blow it at times, but keep affirming him and urging him on, and he will eventually soar! Use your strengths in leadership and decision making to benefit your husband, and believe me, your intimacy levels together will flourish! If you need help with this, contact me and I will coach you.

Being slow to speak involves not pushing back verbally, blaming, justifying, or rationalizing quickly. If you need to, take notes or write down your thoughts. You will have your chance.

Remember that the most important thing at the moment is to love your spouse with listening ears and refrain from giving your input. If you have monopolized the time, be sensitive and seek the other's input to give them a chance. If you have heard them thoroughly, it is okay to ask for a turn to speak.

Make sure your words build your spouse up and don't tear them down. Be respectful. The sad truth is that, more often than not, we treat other people better than we treat our spouse. Shame on us! Stop it! Be quick to listen, slow to speak, and slow get angry. If you feel your partner is about to blow his/her top, activate Coaching Tip #1: use your secret code word!

Even though anger is a normal and good emotion, when anger isn't controlled quickly, it turns into fits of rage or bitterness. You've actually crossed the line.

When you cross the line, God calls that 'sin.' Why? The main reason is because you're not being loving any more. Angry people don't realize that they are hurting their victim deeply. Angry people forget who's around and they hurt innocent bystanders. Angry people aren't listening, except for more ammunition to shoot back with.

Angry people are more interested in the 'win' than the 'win-win.' Angry people aren't showing empathy, they only care about themselves. Angry people aren't seeing the whole picture, they become tunnel-visioned.

Angry people aren't aware of the hurtful words that are coming out of their mouths. Angry people aren't helping the situation, they're actually complicating it. Angry people aren't cognizant that their anger problem will perpetuate to the next generation. So, be slow to get angry!

See No Evil
Initially, I said to "Assume the best in your spouse."
Now I want you to "See the best in your spouse."
Everyone has strengths and weaknesses, even you! Please allow me to paraphrase a question that Jesus asked, "Why do you look at and judge the small imperfections of your spouse, when you have glaring problems within you?

We are quick to see evil and judge one another. Strengths can actually become weaknesses when they are not used in a loving and gracious manner. Weaknesses can easily become strengths when your spouse helps develop them in you.

This is the beauty of a marriage relationship where couples care enough to see the potential in each other, rather than the negative aspects. No longer see the evil, but seize the opportunity to bless and build into one another so your intimacy quotient goes off the charts!

As William A. Ward said, "The pessimist complains about the wind; the optimist expects it to change; the realist adjusts the sails." Be the realist in your marriage and make whatever adjustments are necessary to sail happily into the sunset together!

Seeing no evil actually will give your life a second chance at life! Looking at people, especially your spouse, through gracious eyes takes a huge burden off of you. I get that you might have to sometimes be skeptical and discerning so you don't get taken advantage of in other relationships, but you need to start treating your marriage and your lifetime partner differently – with unconditional love, with extra amounts of grace, and with tender loving care. Take it from me, you will begin thriving emotionally, physically, and even spiritually!

So, Hear No Evil – Speak No Evil – See No Evil! This will truly help reduce fighting in your marriage and jazz it up too!
But if things get out of hand, my advice to you is to "Love 'em & Leave 'em!"

CHAPTER THREE

Love 'em & Leave 'em

The advice sounds counter-intuitive, but even in a boxing match, the referee will send one boxer to their corner in order to give the opponent a breather and to determine whether the fight should continue or not.

Shouldn't we also be cognizant of our partner's need for a break, and because we love 'em, leave 'em for an intentional break? Or if you need to take a break from the intense moment, shouldn't you be able to excuse yourself to love 'em and leave 'em before you do or say something you regret? You bet!

When you see things starting to get out of hand, go to your corner for a time-out and count to ten. Better yet, use the following **Ten Cool-Off Questions** to reflect on your own before you get back into the ring.

These questions will serve two important purposes. First, it will give you time to regain your cool in order to fight fair, it will help you keep the big picture in mind, and it will allow you to engage with all of your faculties.

And secondly, the questions are geared to helping you regain your perspective of the situation so you can maximize the conflict – working towards the 'win-win.'

The Ten Cool-Off Questions

In Appendix B, you will see a shortened version of these questions that you can cut out of the book and post in a strategic place. You can then easily access the list when you need an intentional 'time out.

1. **What's the real issue?** Do I have all the facts? Am I fully aware of the issue at hand? Is fighting over this issue worth the effort and energy we'll use? Is this an issue that we fight about often? If so, how can we finally resolve this so we don't fight about this issue again?

If you're a Christian, here are other questions you can ask; have I prayed for wisdom (James 1:2)? What does the bible teach about this topic (2Timothy 3:16-17)? What is my responsibility in this circumstance (Galatians 6:1-2)?

2. **Why am I impassioned about this issue?** Is this a major problem or a minor one? Was there a trauma either one of us suffered in the past that brings out these feelings? Here are other questions to consider if you are a Christian; am I filled with the Spirit at this moment (Ephesians 5:18)? Am I exhibiting my natural tendencies or the Spirit's fruit (Galatians 5:22-25)? Am I caring about the feelings of my partner (Philippians 2:3-4)?

3. **Is my anger under control?** Why am I angry? Is my response to the problem at hand complicating or calming things? Am I able to control my tone of voice, word choices, and body language? Have I refrained from drinking alcohol or taking drugs that cause me to not think rationally?

As a Christian, am I allowing my anger to cross over the line to sin (Ephesians 4:26-27)? Am I remaining sober-minded (Colossians 3:1-2)? Am I allowing the Spirit to control me rather than my own strength (Philippians 4:13)?

4. **Am I somehow at fault too?** Did I do something after his/her offense that made the situation worse? I know it takes two to tango, so did step on his/her feet accidentally?
Is my ego preventing me from seeing this issue clearly? Even as a Christian, this is a challenging one. Jesus challenges us to not focus on the speck in their eye, but to concentrate on the plank in my own eye (Matthew 7:3-5). Am I doing this?

5. **Are there additional stressors in my life?** Could this issue just be the 'straw that broke the camel's back'? What can I do to relieve some of this stress? Christians experience stress too, so have I stopped to pray and thank the Lord for His presence and peace (Philippians 4:6-7)? Am I looking beyond the stressor to see things from God's perspective (James 1:2-4)? Is there a sin that I need to confess in order to free me from its emotional and physical drain on my body (1 John 1:9)?

6. *Am I ready to forgive? If not, why not?* What's holding me back from extending love and grace to my 'partner in crime?' After I forgive him/her, what steps can we take to ensure that this does not happen again? These questions totally apply for Christians as well, but here's a couple more. Have I already asked God to forgive him/her (Matthew 6:12, 14-15)?
Have I asked God to forgive myself? How many times am I required to forgive him/her (Matthew 18:21-22)?

7. *Am I ready to apologize? If not, why not?* Do I need to eat some 'humble pie' so I can apologize? Do I realize that by apologizing for whatever I did to contribute to this mess will provide an opening for some closure? As Christians, we should always be reminded that humbleness is not a sign of weakness but meekness – quiet confidence. Therefore, shouldn't I be wise and understanding with humility and seek forgiveness? (James

3:13) Shouldn't I also remember that Satan desires to place relational wedges between spouses? (1Peter 5:5-8)

8. *Am I feeling frustrated and hopeless?* Who am I frustrated with more? Do I need to step up my empathy for my partner– what's going on in their life that's contributing to this conflict? Am I willing to do whatever it takes to restore our trust and commitment for each other? As a Christian, am I placing my hope in God (Psalm 42:5)? Am I leaving my frustrations and hurt at the throne of Christ to receive grace and mercy in my time of need (Hebrews 4:16)?

9. *Are my words and actions respectful and edifying?* Am I being respectful of my spouse's efforts and character while voicing concerns over his/her behavior or choices? Am I keeping our conversation 'constructive' rather than 'destructive?' Do I realize that whatever comes out of my mouth can't be taken back? As a Christian wife, do I remember that respecting my husband is my number one responsibility (Ephesians 5:33)?

As a Christian husband, do I remember that my number one responsibility is to love my wife, which includes honoring her for the woman God made her to be (Ephesians 5:25-33)? As a couple, am I remembering to say things that build up rather than disqualify my partner (Ephesians 4:29)?

10. *How will this argument affect others?* First of all, will this affect my spouse negatively or positively? Secondly, are our children going to feel secure or insecure because of this fight? Finally, will I be able to feel good about myself afterwards? As a Christian, the previous questions apply, but here are others. Will

the way we fight be honoring or dishonoring to the name of God (1 Corinthians 10:31)?

Will my children learn how to properly handle tough situations, or will my example be a bad one to pass down to the next generation (Psalm 79:8-10)? Will we handle this in a way that shows we are light and salt in this world (Matthew 5:13-16)?

So, now that you've considered the **Ten Cool-Off Questions**, you should be in a better state of mind to address the concerns at hand. Good job! The next step is to communicate through the issue until it is resolved so it won't have to rear its ugly head again. And if it does, you should be able to settle it quickly by just reiterating what you decided before.

Here's another helpful Coaching Tip…

Coaching Tip #3
One of you should assume the responsibility of taking notes as you go. Create the various lists that come up: the main issue, any side issues, hurt feelings, possible action steps, etc.

This not only will keep the conversation at a good pace (you have to wait for the person to write things down before you continue), but it will also be a good reference for future conversations, as well as a great way to respect the input of one another (writing down what each other says shows that you are truly listening).

See, if you have the 'win-win' in mind, there is wisdom in loving 'em and leaving 'em!

CHAPTER FOUR

Forgive Much?
Instead, be kind to each other, tenderhearted, forgiving one
another, just as God through Christ has forgiven you.
(Ephesians 4:32)

Once upon a time, there were two businessmen who made poor
financial decisions. For the past few years, Bert applied creative
and questionable accounting when he filed his taxes. As a result,
"IRiS" called him in for an audit. As she scrutinized his receipts,
he was sweating bullets in front of her.

She asked a myriad of questions as she worked at reconciling
everything on paper. After what seemed like an entire afternoon,
IRiS finally looked up at Bert and said, you owe Uncle Sam
$130,500.

Would you like to write a check, or use a debit/credit card? His
heart sank. He asked her to explain why. She patiently walked
through everything, showing him where he took too many
liberties. He began to cry and even fell to his knees begging for
mercy.

He didn't have that kind of money and would have to declare
bankruptcy, sell his condo, and his family would have to live in
their car. She looked at her supervisor who was peering in
through her glass door when he heard the commotion. They both
nodded and smiled at each other.

IRiS got up from her desk and asked Bert to sit down. She gave him time to recover and calmly said to him, "Bert, I have good news for you. Every so often, we choose to forgive the tax debt of one person, and we have selected to forgive your $130,500 debt."

Bert couldn't believe what he was hearing, but when it sunk in, he jumped for joy! He gave IRiS a bear hug, thanked her profusely, and ran to his car to tell his wife the unbelievable news!

But on his way home, his friend, Ernie called and asked Bert to meet. It sounded urgent, so Bert agreed. They met at a nearby café, and Ernie looked downcast. Bert asked, "What's wrong, Ernie?" Ernie said, "Bert, I just lost the $3000 I owed you at the races.

I was going to pay you today, but I was feeling lucky, so I went to the track and bet the entire amount on Destiny. If I won, I would've got $300,000! Destiny broke her leg on the first turn, and I went crazy! I couldn't believe it! So, I can't pay you. Can I get another month extension?

Bert was furious! He couldn't believe how stupid Ernie was! "Seriously? You lost the money you owe me on a horse named Destiny? How could you do that? I guess your destiny is I'm going to break your leg too and you're going to pay me double in a month," Bert shouted. He chased him, but Ernie got away.

Ernie went home with his tail between his legs and confessed his blunder to his wife. His wife felt sorry for her husband and did what she could to comfort and support him, even though she didn't agree with what he did too. Afterwards, she called her friend to ask her advice.

She desperately asked, "IRiS, Ernie really blew it today. He lost the $3000 he owed to his friend Bert at the races today. Bert threatened to break his leg and doubled what he owed. What should I do?" IRiS asked, "Did you say he owed money to Bert?" She replied, "That's right." IRiS said, "Don't worry about it. I'll take care of it." So she called Bert and asked him to come back in the office the next day.

Bert came into IRiS' office and started thanking her again for forgiving his debt, and if she ever needed something to not hesitate to ask. But IRiS said to Bert, "I got a call from a dear friend of mine yesterday. She told me that her husband Ernie owed you $3000, but when he asked you for an extension, you threatened to break his leg and doubled his debt."

Bert was speechless and just nodded. "I can't believe you couldn't show your friend the same mercy you received from us just minutes before, and his debt to you was much less than your debt to us was! As a result, we have decided to not forgive your debt and send you to jail for five years. After that, you will have to pay your debt with interest."

Of course this is a contemporary version of Jesus' parable of the Unmerciful Servant in Matthew 18, in which He concludes with, "That's what my heavenly Father will do to you if you refuse to forgive your brothers and sisters from your heart (verse 35)." This was the long way of saying, we need to forgive our spouse when offended.

Forgiving one another is a 'win-win' strategy that jazzes up marriages! But are there erroneous beliefs or myths that prevent us from forgiving freely?

On About.com, I found a great article by *Cherie Burbach, entitled,* *"10 Myths About Forgiveness: Mistaken Beliefs About Forgiving."* Here are her main points in bold, with my comments.

1. You have to get over the feeling of being hurt before you **can forgive.** Not true because unless we offer forgiveness first, the feelings of hurt will linger and it will be a while or possibly never before we are ready to forgive.

2. You shouldn't have to forgive the same thing over and **over.** I wish that were true, but the reality is, habits are hard to break, even with the best intentions. Even Jesus said we should forgive 7x70 times!

3. You can't forgive unless the other person is sorry. That always helps, but taking the higher road is more important for you in the long run.

4. When you forgive, you're saying that what the person did **is okay.** Actually you're forgiving the offense for the sake of maintaining the relationship. The wise next step would be to clearly establish healthy boundaries to prevent the offense from happening again.

5. You should only forgive people you want to stay friends **with.** The longer I live, I realize that peoples' paths often cross again and again. Forgiving people, even though you don't plan on having close ties now, will prevent future encounters from being awkward and uncomfortable.

6. Forgiveness makes you look weak. The opposite is actually true here. It takes courage and strength to grant forgiveness because you are facing your fears and working through hurts.

Forgiving time after time will really develop your character. Even *Ghandi said, "The weak can never forgive. Forgiveness is the attribute of the strong."*

7. Once you forgive a friend, they'll assume they can hurt **you again.** This will occur only if you don't talk through the situation and establish healthy boundaries.

8. Forgiveness gets easier each time you do it. Actually, forgiveness will seem to get easier, but it's the actualization of improved relationships that should be the motivator for resolving issues.

9. Forgiveness naturally comes with time. Time never guarantees anything. It's true that sometimes it feels like things get better over time because you eventually begin to forget it, but rest assured, unless forgiveness takes place, the issues will rear its ugly head again and again. Taking your time to forgive could actually complicate things.

10. You're either a forgiving person, or you're not. Yes, some people are able to forgive more easily than others, but forgiving is a choice, not a personality trait.

Forgiving is the act of love that makes the world a better and healthier place. Now, is it possible to forgive and forget? Personally, I don't think so. There seems to be an emotional closet in our brain that stores the good and bad events in our lives.

They pile and pile up without the ability to push a delete button, unless we experience a concussion and loss of memory, or as we age and develop dementia or Alzheimer's disease.

Until then, these recollections form and shape us into the persons we are today. Don't you wish you could forget some of those things, even things we apologized for or forgave? "Forgive but do not forget, or you will be hurt again. Forgiving changes the perspectives.

Forgetting loses the lesson" (unknown author). On Questions.org, Tim Jackson gives great insight into this dilemma in his article, "Does Forgiving Mean Forgetting?" He said, "It takes greater forgiveness to forgive a grievance that we remember clearly than to forgive a grievance that we have partially forgotten.

Merely ignoring our memory of a grievance isn't forgiveness, it's only suppression of anger. Genuine forgiveness, like God's forgiveness, clearly sees the offense and then forgives it by withdrawing the penalty and continuing the relationship.

It's natural to deal with our anger by suppressing our memory of an offense, but it's supernatural to remember it clearly and renounce our right to revenge. Revenge must be left in the hands of the only One who is always objective and just
(Romans 12:19-21)."

So my admonition for you today as a married couple is to forgive and remember! Remember the things that foster a win-win relationship. In my other book, "Five Ways to 'Jazz Up' Your Marriage," I stated that REMEMBERING Will Jazz Up Your Marriage.

You can read it for a more detailed explanation, but I basically suggested that when you remember your love story, your wedding vows, and your 'firsts' as a couple, this will go a long way to rekindling your heart towards each other.

Here's a list of other things to remember that I jotted down. Can you think of more?

1. Remember, even if you win, you actually lose!
2. Remember, the reason(s) you don't want to forgive, and change them!
3. Remember, you have the opportunity to grow in character when you gift someone with forgiveness
4. Remember, forgiving reboots your relationship
5. Remember, what the hot buttons were and avoid them next time
6. Remember, what their preferences, priorities and principles are
7. Remember, you will need forgiveness in the future
8. Remember, forgiving not only provides a relationship a second chance, it also frees you from becoming bitter and vengeful
9. Remember, forgiving is just the starting point towards your dream marriage
10. Remember, forgiveness is the first step to mending broken hearts
11. Remember, when you forgive or are forgiven, you will be able to sleep better
12. Remember, forgiveness allows communication to flow better
13. Remember, forgiveness is one of the greatest expressions of love you can bless someone with
14. Remember, extending forgiveness is part of seeing the best in someone
15. Remember, when you forgive someone, it will pierce them more than if you gave them a tongue lashing or a piece of your mind – they won't know what just hit them
16. Remember, when you forgive someone, you've made a friend for life
17. Remember, forgiving freely helps your spouse mature and appreciate you more
18. Remember, when you are forgiven, you will forgive others too

19. Remember, forgiveness improves your emotional, spiritual, and physical intimacy

20. Remember, forgiving your spouse doesn't mean that there are no consequences, it just means the relationship is intact to take the next steps

21. Remember, you will still feel the pain of being hurt, betrayed, or violated, but forgiveness will start the healing process from the soul outward

22. Remember, sometimes forgiving someone will take time, but once you get to that point, it's worth the wait

23. Remember, if you've been offended, the offender might not realize it, so don't be afraid to lovingly communicate it

24. Remember, forgiving someone who has already passed is still necessary in order to move on, usually from out of a rut or dysfunction of some sort

25. Remember, if you were abused or violated years ago, you will only be able to unpack the baggage you've been lugging around when you forgive the offender

26. Remember, sometimes your offense costs someone something, so be ready to provide restitution if necessary along with your apology

27. Remember, when you fight it affects others around you too

28. Remember, men don't like to fail, so if they sense their wife will point out a failure, they will either withdraw or get angry

29. Remember, one of the reasons why wives resort to nagging is because they're hoping their husband will eventually hear them and/or their husband will do what they've been asking him to do

These last five are especially for people of faith:

30. Remember, if you don't forgive, God won't forgive you

31. Remember, God forgave you, so you have the supernatural capacity to forgive

32. Remember, forgiveness equals love, and if you love your spouse, the love of God abides in you

33. Remember, as far as it depends on you, live at peace with one another, so forgive him/her

34. Remember, you need to forgive yourself at times – don't allow Satan control over you because of your guilt and shame

Coaching Tip #4
Make and post a sign that says,
"Forgive & Remember."
Forget about forgiving and forgetting.
Forgive and Remember, and Forgive Much!
Are you still 'All In for the Win-Win'?

CHAPTER FIVE

Let's Get Ready to Rumble!
Dr. Gary & Barb Rosberg, America's Family Coaches, created a diagram that helps people, but especially couples 'close the loop' on issues which results in building trust in any hurting relationship.

As imperfect individuals and couples, we all go through times of offending and hurting each other. See diagram on the next page. [Side note: if you are being abused physically, please report it to the appropriate authorities – this will be challenging but helpful for both of you.]

I encourage you to read their book, "Healing the Hurt in Your Marriage" in order to understand this diagram completely, from their heart to yours. But I'm going to use their diagram in a different way.

In another resource, United: *Together in marriage – Together through fire*, by Family Dynamics Institute, they identified 8 Essentials for Marriage:
1. Trust
2. Respect
3. Commitment
4. Support
5. Exceptional Love
6. Emotional Intimacy
7. Spiritual Intimacy
8. Physical Intimacy
For my purposes, I will combine the three types of intimacy and go with **6 Essentials for Marriage**, then use these essentials to close the Rosberg loop.

As you can see, the diagram starts with an offense, which prompts a response – hurt and anger. You then come to a Fork in the Road where you have to choose to deal with the issue or not. Of course, the preferred response is to close the loop by going through the steps with the 'win-win' in mind. Remember, there is no such a thing as a 'short cut' in this process.

Hurt & Anger – Intimacy
Whenever you offend your spouse, your marital intimacy (emotional, spiritual, physical) is affected, and it is now your goal to restore and rebuild it with everything you've got! This is why you must avoid short cuts.

Many times we seek forgiveness right away in order to diffuse the situation without walking through the path to complete resolution. Granted it takes a lot more work, but it's better to contain your wildfire 100% than to let embers smolder to just ignite another fire with the first gust of wind.

1. Once your trust is broken, it takes work to rebuild it, but it's worth it!

2. Depending on how much it has shattered, it might seem impossible to repair, but there is hope – even if it's riding on the coat tail of the hope of your counselor, coach, or friend for a while.

3. If any abuse, addiction, or mental disorder is involved, seek out a health professional to augment you accountability and support team. The goal is to restore your emotional, spiritual, and physical intimacy!

And don't sin by letting anger control you. Don't let the sun go down while you are still angry, for anger gives a foothold to the devil. (Ephesians 4:26-27)

Prepare Hearts – Commitment
The first step in closing the loop is to prepare your hearts with the commitment to resolve the issue and rebuild your trust and intimacy with each other. Here are a few questions to ponder as you prepare your hearts:
1. Are you committed to whatever it takes to work through this?
2. Do you have the 'Win-Win' mindset?
3. Are you careful to not allow your house to be divided?
4. Are you cognizant that one of Satan's schemes is to pit you against each other?
5. Are you willing to invite God into this process through saying a prayer together?
6. Are you committed to God's plan for marriage?
7. Are you committed to your 'ever after'?
8. Can you imagine what your relationship will be like once you resolve this?
9. Have you assembled your support team outside of your marriage?

Therefore I, a prisoner for serving the Lord, beg you to lead a life worthy of your calling, for you have been called by God. (Ephesians 4:1)

Defuse Anger – Exceptional Love
Once you're prepared your hearts, you are now ready to speak with each other calmly, rationally, and sober-mindedly.
This requires exhibiting exceptional love for one another. Here is a list of suggested acts of love you can gift your spouse in this next step:

1. Be empathetic with your partner's circumstances
2. Really try to understanding their point of view
3. Take yourself out of the picture and be more others centered
4. Be sober – no alcohol or drugs allowed
5. Make sure you've established your timeout word in order to diffuse a hostile moment
6. Assume the best in your spouse – they're not intentionally trying to hurt you
7. Act like a duck, you know, let minor comments roll off your back like water on a duck
8. Be ready to apologize for your part in the offense
9. Be ready to forgive when your spouse apologizes
Get rid of all bitterness, rage, anger, harsh words, and slander, as well as all types of evil behavior.
(Ephesians 4:31)

Communicate Concerns – Support
This step is mainly for the one that was 'offended.' He/she should have the freedom to speak openly and honestly about his/ her feelings and complaints without the fear of arguing about it. The 'offender' should demonstrate his/her support by listening and writing down the list of concerns.

Writing the list also demonstrates that the 'offender' heard and understood the concerns. Once the list is complied, I recommend combining similar points together in order to make the list visibly shorter, which provides hope.
1. List all concerns pertaining to the offense
2. Do not comment at this time
3. If side issues come up, just start another list
4. Do not defend at this time
5. Work at writing as many things down as you can but no rationalizing at this time

6. After you have your list, it might look hopeless because of its length
7. Start grouping issues that are related, which shortens the list and provides hope!
8. Give each other a high-five! Good job! You are showing great support for one another. Instead, we will speak the truth in love, growing in every way more and more like Christ, who is the head of his body, the church...Don't use foul or abusive language. Let everything you say be good and helpful, so that your words will be an encouragement to those who hear them.
(Ephesians 4:15 & 29)

Confront Conflict – Trust
Now that all of the concerns are out in the open, although a few more will probably come out as you talk, the 'offender' should be given the freedom to explain themselves humbly, calmly, and constructively. Trust him/her. Seek to hear and see the best in your partner.

The goal, after all is to work through the issues to resolution as best as you can. If you get stuck on one, set an appointment at another time to deal with it.

Here are some helpful tips:
1. Set a time limit for this exercise – you can always return to it later
2. Talk about your rules for fighting – re-read Chapter One – Put Up Your Dukes
3. Review your commitments when you 'prepared your hearts' earlier
4. Resolve one conflict at a time, doing a victory dance after each one

5. If you are having a difficult time resolving an issue, set it aside and take a break – decide when you want to reconvene
6. Avoid avoiding any issue – sweep nothing under the rug
7. Utilize scripture as the final authority on topics without using the bible as a club on each other
8. Remember that even though you seem to be more in the right and in the know, this is not the time to gloat, but to use that knowledge to help the team come to a win-win conclusion
9. After each conflict is confronted and resolved, give each other a chest bump! You just scored! You are rebuilding your trust for and in each other.

Always be humble and gentle. Be patient with each other, making allowance for each other's faults because of your love. Make every effort to keep yourselves united in the Spirit, binding yourselves together with peace. (Ephesians 4:2-3)

Forgive Spouse – Respect
Now that you've done the hard work of lovingly talking through all of the concerns and resolved a good number of them, now is the time to forgive and reconcile. Who should apologize and who should forgive?

Well, it takes two to play tennis, so you can apologize for your own 'faults.' This act is the beginning of building respect for one another.

1. Experiencing all of those wins and victories throughout the process, you will find it much easier to apologize and forgive, and feel good about it!
2. Forgive each other – make out (hug & kiss) as you sincerely make up

3. The fact that you endured through the process will score lots of points towards building and regaining respect for each other
4. Now you will be able to set goals for moving forward, rebuilding trust and intimacy
5. After the goals are set, it's time to get real and practical – agree on actual steps that each person will need to take in order to close the loop(s)
6. Clear boundaries will have to be established as well – a good resource for this is *"Boundaries in Marriage" by Henry Cloud*
7. Decide on an accountability person that will ensure you follow through with the plans – this could involve enlisting a marriage coach
8. Make sure you celebrate after each closed loop – actually including this as one of your steps will serve as motivation
9. Completing the closing the loop process through the many months and years you are together will help build your respect for each other and put the 'happily" in your 'ever after.'

Instead, be kind to each other, tenderhearted, forgiving one another, just as God through Christ has forgiven you.
(Ephesians 4:32)

Rebuild Trust – Intimacy
You will be pleasantly surprised at how much your intimacy levels will improve once you've gone through these 'close the loop' steps. You will:
1. Have constructive and caring conversations
2. Enjoy emotional highs with each victory
3. Smile again and look forward to spending time together
4. Rely on God and each other while working through issues
5. See God really chip away at your imperfections and mature you
6. Witness answers to prayer like never before

7. Desire to 'make love' not war
8. Experience better foreplay
9. Be asked by people why you are so happy
When you and your spouse use the above coaching strategy to continually close the loop when offended, you will simultaneously strengthen each essential of marriage.

That pretty much said it all. Can you see how this can help bring your marriage to the next level of intimacy and get you motivated towards your 'ever after'?

Coaching Tip #5
I highly recommend reading the book by Gary & Barbara Rosberg, "Healing the Hurt in Your Marriage." You should also check out their website for more information about their pro marriage impact around the world at www.americasfamilycoaches.com.

Please also consider joining a Family Dynamic study like, United: Together in marriage – Together through fire interactive study near you. To find out more information got to: http://www.familydynamics.net/united.

CONCLUSION

Back in the Locker Room

Fighting in your marriage is inevitable. Don't feel like you're the only couple that fights – you're not alone. If all you do is fight, then there's a real problem brewing, so seek help from a counselor, pastor, or marriage coach.

Don't be ashamed to ask for help. There are so many people willing and available to get you through your darkest days, offer you options and hope, and to love you through it. Actually fighting isn't all bad if you maximize it for positive impact.

If you didn't notice, boxers, wrestlers, and MMA fighters are always in great shape! They work out and train for positive results. They win some, they lose some, but they are always ready to get in the ring for more in order to become better.

Likewise, married couples have the potential to grow their marriage relationship to greater proportions when they go through the process of constructive conflict. But couples must have the 'win-win' in mind, not just a tie, but both coming out of the ring as winners!

As you noticed, I really kept the book as practical as possible, noting many biblical principles and passages in the End Notes. I believe that any couple will be able to benefit from the information and processes outlined in this book, but Christians should benefit even more.

Not only because relevant bible verses were being applied to marital situations, but because they have access to the Holy Spirit who is waiting to be drawn upon for wisdom and strength to lovingly fight with the 'win-win' in mind. This Holy Person of the Godhead is still available to anyone who chooses to place their faith and lives in God's hands as well as the finished work of Jesus Christ on the cross at Calvary.

If you are not a Christian, would you consider becoming one in order to have a power outside of yourselves available that can help you in life and love? If you are already a Christian, are you taking advantage of the power within you, the Holy Spirit, who wants to bless your socks off?

In either case, when you keep the 'win-win' in mind for your marriage relationship and you utilize these five ways, you will definitely reduce fighting in your marriage and will jazz it up too!

Coaching Tip #6
I highly recommend that you check out Christianity and all it has to offer. I realize that some Christians that you know don't represent the faith too well, but don't let that hinder you from experiencing all that God has for you. Trust me, He will jazz up your life and marriage!

To summarize,
the Five Ways to Reduce Fighting in Your Marriage are:
1. Fight with the Win-Win in Mind
2. Hear No Evil, Speak No Evil, See No Evil
3. Love 'em & Leave 'em
4. Forgive One Another
5. Fight to Close the Loop

It has been a pleasure being part of your life during the reading of this book. It is my heart's desire that you and your forever partner will enjoy jazzed up years together, one special moment at a time.

As much as you think about your passion in life – what God designed and called you to be and do – think about your spouse, marriage, and legacy. Be intentional about growing your love through the seasons of life and thrive! You'll be glad you did!

Did you enjoy this publication?
Visit us online at

www.2ndEmpireMedia.Com
for more unique books and audios